OSTRICHES

by Thane Maynard

Content Adviser:
The Zoological Society
of San Diego

Published in the United States of America by The Child's World®
PO Box 326 • Chanhassen, MN 55317-0326
800-599-READ • www.childsworld.com

PHOTO CREDITS
© Charles Philip Cangialosi/Corbis: 17
© Daniel J. Cox/www.naturalexposures.com: 14
© Frans Lanting/Minden Pictures: 19, 23
© Joe McDonald/Corbis: cover, 1
© Juergen & Christine Sohns/Animals Animals–Earth Scenes: 5
© Leonard Rue Enterprises/Animals Animals–Earth Scenes: 15
© Martin Harvey/Corbis: 6–7
© Martin Harvey/Gallo Images/Corbis: 25
© Nicholas DeVore/Getty Images: 28–29
© OSF/Peter Lillie/Animals Animals-Earth Scenes: 27
© Paul van Gaalen/zefa/Corbis: 8–9
© Roger Tidman/Corbis: 13
© Steve Kaufman/Corbis: 20–21
© Vasily Fedosenko/Reuters/Corbis: 24
© Wally Bauman/Alamy: 11

ACKNOWLEDGMENTS
The Child's World®: Mary Berendes, Publishing Director;
Katherine Stevenson, Editor

The Design Lab: Kathleen Petelinsek, Design and Page Production

LIBRARY OF CONGRESS CATALOGING-IN-PUBLICATION DATA
Maynard, Thane.
  Ostriches / by Thane Maynard.
    p. cm. — (New naturebooks)
  Includes bibliographical references and index.
  ISBN 1-59296-645-4 (library bound : alk. paper)
  1. Ostriches—Juvenile literature. I. Title. II. Series.
  QL696.S9M39 2006
  598.5'24—dc22   2006001373

Table of Contents

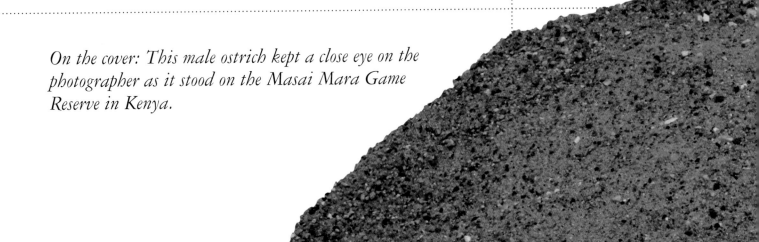

On the cover: This male ostrich kept a close eye on the photographer as it stood on the Masai Mara Game Reserve in Kenya.

Meet the Ostrich!

Ostriches have been around for over 70 million years.

Wild ostriches live only in Africa today, but they once lived in Europe and Asia as well. People raise ostriches on farms all over the world.

The afternoon sun beats down on the plains of Africa. Animals are moving slowly in the heat, searching for food or a place to rest. A giraffe is stretching its long neck to reach juicy leaves high in a tree. Zebras and antelope are munching on low grasses. Nearby, a huge, awkward-looking bird with long legs and a long neck walks slowly along. It pauses and looks around carefully, then dips its long neck to pluck at something on the ground. What could this strange-looking bird be? It's an ostrich!

This female ostrich is walking in the Samburu Game Reserve in Kenya. The reserve is a protected area about 200 miles (322 km) north of the city of Nairobi.

What Do Ostriches Look Like?

Ostriches have the biggest eyes of any land animal—almost 2 inches (5 cm) across. In fact they're bigger than the ostrich's brain! Thick eyelashes help protect the eyes from blowing sands and dust.

Ostriches are outrageous! Everything about these giant birds is oversized, outstretched, and outstanding. Ostriches are the biggest birds in the world. In fact, they are taller and heavier than most people. They stand over 6 feet (2 m) tall and weigh about 250 pounds (113 kg)!

Ostriches have few feathers on their long necks and legs. Their bare skin ranges from pinkish gray in females to pink or blue in males. Their heads are small, and their eyes are large, with long eyelashes.

Here a male ostrich walks slowly on an African plain.

Male and female ostriches look different, but they are both good at hiding. Wild ostriches live in Africa's dry, open areas, including the grasslands called **savannas**. The females, called *hens*, are a brownish gray. This protective coloring, or **camouflage**, makes them hard to see in the open savanna, especially during the day. Baby ostriches are the same brownish color. Males are black, with white feathers on their wings and tail. The male's coloring isn't as good for hiding during the day, but it's great for hiding at night.

You can see the difference in coloring between this male (left) and female (right) as they walk with their chicks in Kenya.

Male ostriches show off their bold coloring when they are trying to attract a hen. The males wave and shake their wings and move their tails up and down.

What Are Ostrich Feathers Like?

In the 1700s and 1800s, shipping and selling ostrich feathers was big business! The male's long white feathers, called *plumes*, were especially popular for decorating hats. Around 1914 to 1918, fashions changed, and long plumes on hats were no longer popular.

Ostrich feathers are different from those of other birds. Most birds have a light coating of oil on their feathers to make the feathers waterproof. They also have stiff **flight feathers** on their wings and tails to help them to fly. Ostriches can't fly, so they don't have stiff flight feathers. Instead, all their feathers are soft and fluffy. Their feathers aren't waterproof, either. Like other birds, ostriches use their beaks to clean and groom their feathers, or **preen**.

People have used ostrich feathers on clothing and hats for at least 5,000 years. In the 1700s and 1800s, the feathers were so popular that ostriches were hunted too heavily and almost died out. People started raising ostriches on farms instead.

Ostrich feathers like these are very soft. Can you imagine what it would feel like to run your hands across an ostrich's wing?

How Fast Can Ostriches Run?

When an ostrich runs, its footsteps can be up to 16 feet (5 m) apart!

Ostriches are the second-fastest land animal. Cheetahs are the fastest—they can run at 60 miles (97 km) per hour, although not for long.

Ostriches can't fly, but they make up for it by running really fast! In fact, they're the fastest animals on two legs. They can run 40 miles (64 km) per hour, for hours at a time. The fastest human track star can run only 24 miles (39 km) per hour, and only for the 100-meter dash!

Many **predators** such as lions run fast so they can catch other animals for dinner. Since ostriches eat mostly plants, these giant birds don't run to catch their dinner. In fact, they run to keep from being somebody else's dinner! Lions and hyenas love to eat ostriches if they can catch them.

These ostriches were frightened by the photographer as they stood by a lake in Kenya. The picture had to be taken quickly before all the birds ran away!

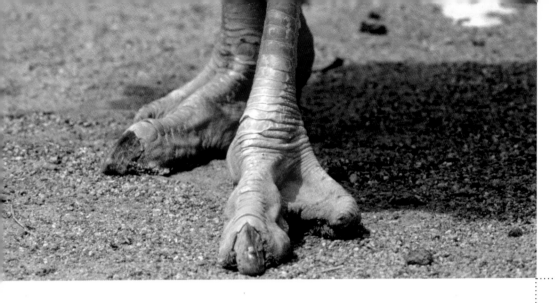

Here is a close-up view of an ostrich's two-toed feet.

How do ostriches run so fast? Besides their long legs, just look at their feet! These sturdy feet are strong enough to carry around a 250-pound animal all day. Most birds have four toes on each foot, and some have three. Ostriches, though, have only two. The toes provide a good grip so the ostrich can run really fast. The ostrich's claws, which are about 4 inches (10 cm) long, dig in just like the spikes on a baseball shoe.

Almost all birds have hollow, lightweight bones that make them light enough to fly. Ostriches don't fly, but they still have hollow bones. Their leg bones are gigantic—as big as horse or cow bones. But even these big bones are hollow.

Ostriches use their wings to balance their bodies as they run.

Sometimes ostriches run in circles, making it easier to catch them when they try to run away.

You can see the huge bones in this male's legs as he walks in the Kalahari Desert.

What Do Ostriches Eat?

Ostriches don't have teeth. Like many other birds, they swallow sand and small pebbles that help grind up their food once they've eaten it.

Ostriches rarely need to drink water. They get most of the water they need from the foods they eat.

Ostriches aren't picky eaters. They eat a wide variety of plant shoots, leaves, flowers, and seeds. They also eat bugs, and sometimes lizards! Animals that eat both plants and animals are called **omnivores**. Bears, raccoons, and people are omnivores, too.

Ostriches use their wide beaks to scoop food off the ground. Like many birds, they don't swallow one leaf or seed at a time. Instead, they collect the food in their throat, or **crop**, until it is about the size of a baseball. Then they swallow the whole lump. Their necks are so long, you can watch the bulge go down as they swallow!

This ostrich found a leafy fern to eat. It tore at the leaf several times, biting off small bits until nothing was left.

How Do Ostriches Protect Themselves?

Just one kick from an ostrich can kill a lion.

Ostriches also have claws on their wingtips that they can use to protect themselves.

Ostriches would rather run than fight, especially when they're facing something like a hungry lion. But ostriches' claws and powerful legs aren't just for running away. Those strong leg muscles help the birds kick very hard! In fact, they are one of the hardest-kicking animals in the world. They are especially brave about protecting their young. A mother ostrich will even pretend to be hurt to draw lions or hyenas away from her nest or babies.

You can see the powerful muscles in this female's legs as she runs away from the photographer in the Kalahari Desert.

Ostriches live in small groups, often with about 10 birds. Ostriches are always watching for danger. Their sharp eyesight usually helps them see danger in time to run away or protect their young. Ostriches also have good hearing and listen carefully to all the sounds around them.

Many people think that frightened ostriches hide their heads in the sand or dirt. That isn't true! If an ostrich senses danger and can't run away, it drops to the ground, lays its head and neck flat on the ground, and stays completely still. Since its head and neck are the same color as the ground, it might look from a distance as though the head and neck are underground.

Ostrich groups are sometimes larger—up to 100 members.

Ostriches often feed near other animals such as zebras and antelope. The ostriches' keen eyesight and hearing help keep the other animals safe, and the other animals stir up bugs and other creatures the ostriches like to eat.

This female is guarding her eggs and has laid her neck flat on the ground. Imagine that you were standing behind the sand dune. If you were watching from behind the sand dune, she might look as if she didn't have a head or had buried it in the sand.

How Are Baby Ostriches Born?

The hen's brown coloring hides her when she guards the nest during the day. The male's black coloring hides him when he guards it at night.

An ostrich egg weighs about 3 pounds (a little over 1 kg), or as much as 24 chicken eggs.

Ostrich hens can recognize their own eggs even when they are mixed in with the eggs of other hens.

Ostrich groups often have one male and several hens. There is one "main hen," who mates with the male first. The male scrapes out a shallow nest on the ground, and the main hen lays about a dozen eggs in it. She doesn't lay them all at the same time. Instead, she usually lays an egg every other day for about three weeks. The other hens also lay their eggs in the same nest. Only the male and the main hen take turns sitting on the nest. The female sits on the nest during the day, and the male takes his turn at night.

This female is watching over a nest full of eggs in Botswana. Lots of predators would eat the eggs if they had the chance.

Here you can see an ostrich chick as it hatches from its egg.

About 45 days later, the baby ostriches, called *chicks*, hatch. Not all of the eggs hatch. Even so, with so many hens laying their eggs in one nest, there can be 15 to 60 babies! Many other baby birds can't walk or fly right after they hatch, but ostrich chicks begin walking and pecking the ground for food right away. Ostrich chicks usually hatch during Africa's rainy season, so there are often lots of bugs, flowers, and tender new leaves for the chicks to eat.

Even with the adults guarding them, many of the chicks are caught and eaten by predators such as vultures, jackals, and hyenas. Those that survive grow quickly. In fact, they grow almost 1 foot (30 cm) a month for their first few months.

Among some African tribes, empty ostrich eggshells were used for storing water.

Ostrich chicks are very hungry and tend to eat anything they see.

These ostrich chicks were very curious about the photographer's camera. Shortly after this photograph was taken, the chick in front pecked the camera to be sure it wasn't food!

25

How Do Ostriches Communicate?

Ostriches also make a variety of sounds, including a hissing roar. When male ostriches are protecting their territory or trying to attract a mate, they make a deep booming sound.

Sometimes ostriches look as if they are dancing. But they're not dancing for fun, the way people do. Instead, they are communicating with each other. During breeding season, a male tries to keep other males out of the area, or **territory**, in which he lives. He chases away other males by strutting around and flicking his wings.

Ostriches have a "pecking order" within their group. Those that are higher in the pecking order get their own way, and those that are lower in the pecking order give in to them. The ostriches use their bodies to communicate who's in charge. An ostrich that intends to get its own way holds its head, wings, and tail feathers high. An ostrich that is giving way droops these body parts instead.

Here you can see two male ostriches fighting over a territory. When they fight, male ostriches kick and hiss at each other, and flap and fluff their wings to look bigger and stronger.

What Does the Future Hold for Ostriches?

Ostriches can live to be about 50 years old.

Ostriches are very curious—especially about shiny objects. They will peck and peck at a shiny object to figure out what it is. People who raise ostriches are careful not to wear jewelry or glasses around them!

Today, there are something like two million ostriches in the world. On farms, they are raised for their meat, eggs, and feathers, as well as for their skin. The skin is made into expensive leather for boots, belts, and other products.

In the wild, ostriches fit perfectly into Africa's balance of nature. Many people are working to protect the parks and **wildlife reserves** where ostriches live. Right now, the future of ostriches looks good—and there are lots of people interested in keeping it that way!

This group of ostriches is watching for danger as the sun sets on the African plain.

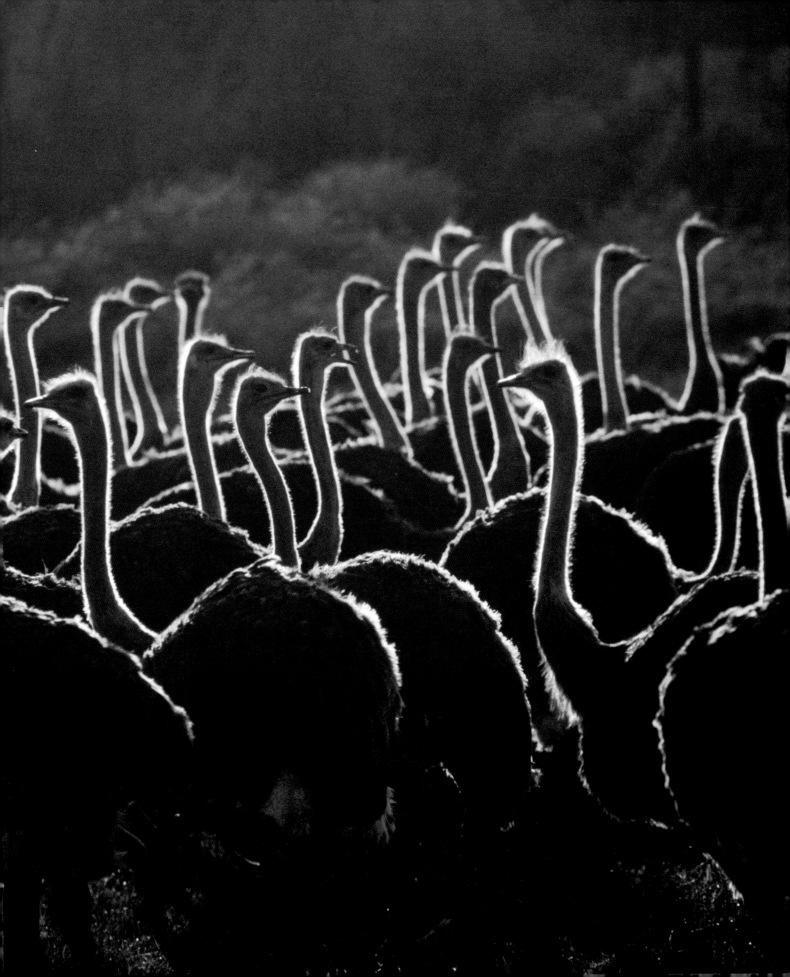

Glossary

camouflage (KA-muh-flazh) Camouflage is special coloring or markings that help an animal blend in with its surroundings. Ostrich females and babies are camouflaged by their brownish gray color.

crop (KROP) In birds, a crop is a pouchlike area in the bird's throat where it holds food before swallowing it. Ostriches have crops.

flight feathers (FLYT FEH-thurz) Flight feathers are stiff feathers that most birds have in their wings and tails to help them fly. Ostriches don't fly, and they have soft, fluffy feathers instead.

omnivores (OM-nih-vorz) Omnivores are animals that eat both plants and animals. Ostriches are omnivores.

predators (PRED-uh-terz) Predators are animals that hunt and kill other animals for food. Some predators, such as lions and hyenas, eat ostriches.

preen (PREEN) When birds preen their feathers, they slide their beaks along the feathers to clean and tidy them. Like all birds, ostriches preen.

savanna (suh-VA-nuh) A savanna is a grassland with scattered trees and shrubs. African savannas are home to ostriches and many other animals.

territory (TEHR-uh-tor-ee) An animal's territory is the area that the animal claims as its own and defends against outsiders. Male ostriches have territories.

wildlife reserves (WILD-life rih-ZURVZ) Wildlife reserves are areas set aside for wild animals. Some ostriches in Africa live in wildlife reserves.

To Find Out More

Read It!

Aardema, Verna, and Marcia Brown (illustrator). *How the Ostrich Got Its Long Neck: A Tale from the Akamba of Kenya.* New York: Scholastic, 1995.

Arnold, Caroline. *Ostriches and Other Flightless Birds.* Minneapolis, MN: Carolrhoda, 1990.

Elwood, Ann. *Ostriches and Other Ratites.* Poway, CA: Wildlife Education, 2002.

On the Web

Visit our home page for lots of links about ostriches:
http://www.childsworld.com/links

Note to Parents, Teachers, and Librarians: We routinely check our Web links to make sure they're safe, active sites—so encourage your readers to check them out!

Index

About the Author

Thane Maynard is the vice president of public information at the Cincinnati Zoo & Botanical Garden. He is best known as a writer and host of numerous wildlife programs, including the daily public radio series The 90-Second Naturalist. *Mr. Maynard has been featured on* Good Morning America, Today, *and* CBS This Morning *and has been a regular wildlife expert on* Late Night with Conan O'Brien. *He works with numerous conservation programs, including the World Wildlife Fund (WWF), Conservation International, and The Nature Conservancy.*